To

From

THANKS FOR BEING MY FRIEND

Thanks for Being My Friend

Judy Harper Spaar
(and friends)

**Andrews McMeel
Publishing**

Kansas City

99 00 01 02 03 BIN 10 9 8 7 6 5 4 3 2 1

www.andrewsmcmeel.com

Book design by Lisa Martin

Library of Congress Cataloging-in-Publication Data
Spaar, Judy.
    Thanks for being my friend / by Judy Spaar (and friends).
      p.   cm.
    ISBN 0-8362-8297-3 (pbk.)
    1. Female friendship.   2. Women—Psychology.   I. Title.
BF575.F66S63   1999
177'.62'082—dc21   98-53691
                                     CIP

ACKNOWLEDGMENTS

Thank you to everyone
who contributed to this book:

Polly Blair
Jennifer Fox
Jessica Kerrigan
Elizabeth Nuelle
Shana Watts

INTRODUCTION

Best girlfriends! They're our movie buddies, our
partners in giggle fests, our soul mates, and our
confidantes. They define who we are and help
us find our place in life. They share every big
moment, along with hundreds of tiny ones.
They make us laugh, they tell us the honest
truth, and they know when to listen and when
to offer advice. How could we make it through
the day if we couldn't call our best friend on
the phone and tell her every detail? We make
lots of friends throughout our lives, but we
reserve a special place in our heart for our best

friend. This book is in tribute to that friend in my life.

I hope you and your friends enjoy laughing and reminiscing over the situations I have recalled for this book and that it helps you appreciate that magical bond we call friendship.

—Judy Harper Spaar

THANKS FOR

knowing when to listen.

THANKS FOR

calling on my child's first

day of kindergarten and

understanding why

I was crying.

•
•
•
2

Thanks for bringing
over coffee and
croissants on
Saturday mornings.

Thanks for walking
me home after my
first college party.

THANKS FOR

crying with me during

sad movies, then laughing

about it afterward.

THANKS FOR

staying and helping me

clean up after our big

Christmas party.

Thanks for loaning me
your favorite dress
for my class reunion.

Thanks for
not expecting a thing.

THANKS FOR

the five dollars

you loaned me.

THANKS FOR

the Saturday afternoon

shopping excursions.

Thanks for
holding the bouquet
at my wedding.

Thanks for calling
at 11:00 at night
just to make sure my
child was making it
through the chicken pox.

THANKS FOR

understanding

before I say a word.

THANKS FOR

our hilarious

girls' nights out.

Thanks for
loaning me your
handkerchief at
my child's baptism.

Thanks for going
streaking with me
at midnight during
my seventh-grade
slumber party.

THANKS FOR

bringing over dinner

on my first night home

with my new baby.

THANKS FOR

filling in at Lamaze class

when my husband

was out of town.

Thanks for
the long talks.

●
●
●

Thanks for
the surprise
birthday party.

THANKS FOR

making me laugh.

21

THANKS FOR

trumping my ace when

we're bridge partners.

Thanks for
the phone calls.

Thanks for buying
Girl Scout cookies from
my daughter every year.

THANKS FOR

helping me get over *him*.

THANKS FOR

driving me to work when

my car broke down.

Thanks for
not caring when
I yell too loudly
at football games.

Thanks for
going with me
to summer camp.

THANKS FOR

feeding my cat and

watering my plants when

I went on vacation.

THANKS FOR

taking that cruise

with me.

30

Thanks for
helping me plant
my herb garden.

Thanks for
the recipes.

THANKS FOR

helping me remove the slats

from our summer camp

counselor's bed.

THANKS FOR

sharing your goodies bag from

home during college finals.

34

Thanks for going to the hair salon with me the morning of senior prom.

Thanks for being my
college roommate.

THANKS FOR

covering for me

Saturday morning when

my Mom called and I

was still out.

THANKS FOR

giving me my first perm.

Thanks for
helping me make
my child's
Halloween costume.

Thanks for trying out for
cheerleading with me.

THANKS FOR

going through

sorority rush with me.

THANKS FOR

sending me flowers.

Thanks for
loving me
just the way
I am.

Thanks for bringing
the cookies and chips
on our road trips.

THANKS FOR

not letting go of my hand

when we went through

haunted houses.

THANKS FOR

not making me feel like a

third wheel when I go to dinner

with you and your husband.

●
●
●

Thanks for
making me
feel special.

Thanks for
crying with me
when Elvis died.

THANKS FOR

taking horseback riding

lessons with me.

THANKS FOR

having the guts to

tell me that I was in

an abusive relationship.

Thanks for
being the most
honest person
I know.

Thanks for sharing
your bug repellent
at summer camp.

THANKS FOR

sharing your dreams, fears,

and chocolate with me.

THANKS FOR

bringing me

back to reality.

Thanks for giving me
something to
look forward to.

Thanks for
trying new lunch
spots with me.

THANKS FOR

always knowing the

right thing to say.

THANKS FOR

reading great books

and then loaning

them to me.

Thanks for
watching the kids so
my husband and I could
go out on a date.

Thanks for
the baby clothes.

THANKS FOR

helping with

my garage sale.

THANKS FOR

never saying

"I told you so."

Thanks for
accepting me
for who I am.

Thanks for being
my biggest fan.

THANKS FOR

taking notes in class

when I overslept.

THANKS FOR

loaning me your car.

Thanks for
keeping me awake
in art history class.

Thanks for
helping me fine-tune
my tennis serve.

THANKS FOR

dropping by just to say "hi!"

THANKS FOR

coming to my child's

T-ball tournament.

Thanks for
popping popcorn
just before the
video starts.

Thanks for asking
about my family.

THANKS FOR

not being angry

when I don't call

for a few weeks.

THANKS FOR

giving my son his

first Barney doll.

Thanks for giving
my daughter her
first Barbie doll.

Thanks for complimenting me on my new hairstyle.

THANKS FOR

laughing at my jokes.

THANKS FOR

bringing the salad

to my dinner party.

Thanks for wiping
the spots off the wine
glasses before the other
guests arrived.

Thanks for sharing
the late-night pizzas.

THANKS FOR

loaning me sunscreen

at the pool.

THANKS FOR

comforting me when my

cat died and surprising

me with a new one.

Thanks for going
with me to hear our
favorite jazz band on
Thursday nights.

Thanks for fixing
PB&Js for the kids
and not minding the
mess they make.

THANKS FOR

always being there.

THANKS FOR

sharing your makeup

tips with me.

Thanks for
helping me move.

Thanks for proofreading
my essays in college.

THANKS FOR

letting me listen to country

music in the car even though

you can't stand it.

THANKS FOR

calling and making my

entire day brighter.

Thanks for making
curtains for my new
house then helping
me hang them.

Thanks for
making my world
a better place.

THANKS FOR

being my strictest confidante.

THANKS FOR

never being condescending.

Thanks for helping
me with my child's
birthday party.

Thanks for bringing
over my favorite ice cream,
then eating it straight from
the carton with me.

THANKS FOR

French-braiding my hair.

THANKS FOR

sending me to the spa for

a pedicure when I was

eight months pregnant.

Thanks for taping
the last episode of
Seinfeld for me.

Thanks for going
apartment hunting
with me.

THANKS FOR

hiring a male stripper for

my thirtieth birthday party.

THANKS FOR

inviting me over

for the holidays.

Thanks for
going to Florida
on Spring Break
with me.

Thanks for always having my favorite soda in the fridge.

THANKS FOR

buying in-line skates and

learning to skate with me.

THANKS FOR

walking barefoot in

the park with me on

our lunch hour.

Thanks for loaning
me your umbrella.

Thanks for introducing
me to the man who turned
out to be my husband.

THANKS FOR

picking me up at the airport.

THANKS FOR

knowing I like cream

and sugar in my coffee.

Thanks for listening
when I need to vent.

Thanks for teaching me
how to shave my legs when
we were growing up.

THANKS FOR

taking me out on my birthday.

113

THANKS FOR

wishing me a

Happy Mother's Day

the day my child

was born.

Thanks for never
dating any of my
ex-boyfriends.

Thanks for telling me
you weren't asleep when
I needed you at 1:00 A.M.

THANKS FOR

joining the health

club with me.

THANKS FOR

letting me cry on

your shoulder.

Thanks for throwing
me a baby shower.

Thanks for your
Christmas letters.

THANKS FOR

going with me to

the all-night coffee shop

during college finals.

THANKS FOR

helping me study for

my master's degree.

Thanks for the hugs.

Thanks for getting
me that job.

THANKS FOR

inviting me to join

your bunco group.

THANKS FOR

carpooling our kids

to school.

Thanks for watching *Grease* with me again.

Thanks for being
my first friend
when we moved into
the neighborhood.

THANKS FOR

sticking up for me

on the playground

in grade school.

THANKS FOR

playing dress-up with me

when we were kids.

Thanks for the
home-baked goodies.

Thanks for not
grimacing in pain when
I sing in the car.

THANKS FOR

helping me refinish

my grandmother's

old armoire.

THANKS FOR

giving me the first tree

for my new yard.

Thanks for staying up
with me to watch
Gone With the Wind.

Thanks for the
housewarming gift when
my husband and I built
our first home.

THANKS FOR

waiting for me

after school.

THANKS FOR

driving me to and

from school in your

new convertible.

Thanks for never
leaving me out of
a conversation.

Thanks for
holding my hand
when I got my
first tattoo.

THANKS FOR

encouraging me to apply

for a better job.

THANKS FOR

helping me find the

perfect little black dress

for the office party.

Thanks for sharing my
locker in high school.

Thanks for not always
giving me advice.

THANKS FOR

helping me clean

my apartment before

I moved in.

THANKS FOR

telling me there was

toilet paper stuck

to my shoe.

Thanks for taking my
dog to the vet.

Thanks for
always inviting me
to go along.

THANKS FOR

the funny scrapbook

you put together of our

weekend getaway.

THANKS FOR

helping me walk with

crutches when I broke

my leg skiing.

Thanks for watching our favorite soap with me.

Thanks for sending me get-well cards when I'm home sick.

THANKS FOR

helping me learn

to surf the Net.

THANKS FOR

bringing me lunch

when I didn't have time

to leave my desk.

Thanks for sending
me regular E-mails to
keep me updated on
your busy life.

Thanks for listening
to me obsess over my
crush for hours.

THANKS FOR

going to the hospital with

me when I got stitches.

THANKS FOR

being there when my

boyfriend dumped me.

Thanks for buying me
that shirt that I never
paid you back for.

Thanks for looking at
old photos and scrapbooks
and crying with me.

THANKS FOR

baby-sitting with me even

though we missed the biggest

party of the year.

THANKS FOR

talking to me on the first

day of kindergarten.

Thanks for staying up
at night and watching
old movies with me
when I couldn't sleep.

Thanks for
remembering.

THANKS FOR

your smile of reassurance

when I need it most.

THANKS FOR

taking me to that new coffee

place and helping me learn

to order a "vanilla-double-

iced-skinny-decaf latte!"

Thanks for being my
source of strength when
my mom passed away.

Thanks for being the
sister I never had.

THANKS FOR

kicking me under the table

when I was about to say

something stupid.

THANKS FOR

trying out new nail

polish with me.

Thanks for being the
most entertaining "aunt"
my children could have.

Thanks for
caring about what's
important to me.

THANKS FOR

rushing across town to

get me when my car

ran out of gas.

THANKS FOR

watching fireworks with

me on the Fourth of July.

Thanks for eating
watermelon with me
and seeing how far we
could spit the seeds.

Thanks for whispering
with me in class when the
teacher's back was turned.

THANKS FOR

helping me paint the backdrop

for the kids' school play.

THANKS FOR

dragging me to the gym

with you so I wouldn't sit

around feeling fat.

●
●
●

Thanks for giving me
stationery on my
birthday so I'll be sure
to keep in touch.

Thanks for
buying Absolut
instead of Smirnoff.

THANKS FOR

understanding my

mood swings.

THANKS FOR

catching fireflies with

me on summer nights

in the backyard when

we were kids.

Thanks for
reminding me
that life goes on
after divorce.

Thanks for helping me
stay on my diet.

THANKS FOR

going with me to see the

latest chick flick when my

husband wouldn't go.

THANKS FOR

going out of your way

to be nice.

Thanks for taking night classes with me.

Thanks for telling me
how my new dress
really looked.

THANKS FOR

taking me to the hospital

to visit my mother

when she was ill.

THANKS FOR

telling me that my boyfriend

made a pass at you.

Thanks for being
my sounding board.

Thanks for getting
my prescription filled when
I was too sick to drive.

THANKS FOR

going swimsuit shopping

with me.

THANKS FOR

sharing your recipe for

chocolate chip cookies.

Thanks for telling
me my miniskirt was
too short before my
blind date arrived.

Thanks for going
to that estate sale
and finding the coolest
jewelry for my birthday.

THANKS FOR

helping me choose my

wedding dress.

THANKS FOR

being there for me

when my husband was

in the hospital.

Thanks for picking up
the phone when you
hear me on your answering
machine, especially when
you're screening your calls.

Thanks for your quiet
confidence in me.

200

THANKS FOR

helping me write thank-you

notes after my wedding shower.

THANKS FOR

camping out all night with

me so we could get the

best concert seats.

Thanks for loaning me
"something borrowed"
for my wedding.

Thanks for
throwing me a party
when I finally received
my master's degree.

THANKS FOR

always having the coffee on.

THANKS FOR

letting me stay with you

when the snowstorm

left me without electricity

for three days.

Thanks for coming
over at 2 A.M. to stay
with my child when
I went into labor.

Thanks for
always telling
me first.

THANKS FOR

taping our soap opera then

telling me what happens.

THANKS FOR

remembering our locker

combination in high school

when I forgot it.

Thanks for never
freaking out, no matter
what I tell you I've done.

Thanks for being
my partner when we
started our own
business together.

THANKS FOR

ironing my skirt when I was

late for my job interview.

THANKS FOR

giving me a glowing

recommendation when

my prospective boss

called you for one.

Thanks for being my
movie buddy.

Thanks for always
being glad I called.

216

THANKS FOR

telling me I looked good

two days after my

baby was born.

THANKS FOR

always telling me what

I need to hear.

Thanks for helping me plan our ten-year high school class reunion.

Thanks for helping
me find the perfect
furniture for my
child's dorm room.

THANKS FOR

making it fun to be a

football widow.

THANKS FOR

always giving me a beautiful

ornament at Christmastime.

Thanks for referring me to a good, honest mechanic.

Thanks for getting your
ears pierced with me.

THANKS FOR

running to Taco Bell

with me at midnight.

THANKS FOR

helping me shop for

my new car.

Thanks for
being the best neighbor
I've ever had.

Thanks for
helping me wrap
Christmas presents.

THANKS FOR

touching my heart.

THANKS FOR

never losing your

temper with me.

Thanks for telling me
when you're angry or
upset so we can
talk it through.

Thanks for going
with me to traffic court
when I fought my
speeding ticket.

THANKS FOR

always coming to tell

me when you were leaving

the playground when

we were kids.

THANKS FOR

calling to tell me when

there is a great movie

on television.

Thanks for
worrying
about me.

Thanks for noticing
even the smallest change
in my mood and
questioning the reason.

THANKS FOR

dancing around like a

crazy person with me when

my child finally used

the potty-chair.

THANKS FOR

suggesting the best,

quickest summer dinners.

Thanks for telling me
the best jokes.

Thanks for helping me
write my ad for the singles
section of the classifieds.

THANKS FOR

putting our dinner bill

on your charge card when

I didn't have any cash.

THANKS FOR

getting me a subscription to

New Yorker magazine.

Thanks for bringing me frozen yogurt when I had my wisdom teeth pulled.

Thanks for
helping me organize
the church bazaar.

THANKS FOR

buying me a year of

diaper service when

I had my twins.

THANKS FOR

being my calm in the storm.

246

Thanks for being my campaign manager when I ran for office.

Thanks for
giving me comfort
and strength.

THANKS FOR

standing up with me

when I renewed my

wedding vows.

THANKS FOR

buying double pictures.

Thanks for
watching my kids on
our anniversary.

Thanks for
clueing me in on
office politics.

THANKS FOR

needlepointing a pillow

for my baby.

253

THANKS FOR

making my over-the-hill

party the perfect beginning

to the forty-somethings.

Thanks for always calculating the tip when we go out to lunch.

Thanks for
going to aerobics
classes with me.

THANKS FOR

helping me find my keys.

THANKS FOR

waiting to make sure my car

starts before driving away.

Thanks for
making the guacamole
for my holiday party.

Thanks for
supporting me
when I started
dating again.

THANKS FOR

always asking how my

family is doing.

THANKS FOR

showing me how yummy

pineapple and Canadian

bacon pizzas are.

Thanks for surprising me
with tickets to the sold-out
Janet Jackson concert.

Thanks for helping me
dye eggs for the church
Easter egg hunt.

THANKS FOR

unloading the dishwasher.

THANKS FOR

mailing me funny cards

for no reason at all.

Thanks for
telling me when
I have lipstick
on my teeth.

Thanks for saving
the top of my wedding
cake in your freezer then
giving it to my husband
and me on our first
anniversary.

THANKS FOR

going to garage sales

with me.

269

THANKS FOR

buying me a

hummingbird

feeder.

Thanks for
working the concession
stand with me at
the local fair.

Thanks for always
wearing a watch so
we're never late.

THANKS FOR

helping me piece together

photos for the video

commemorating my parents'

fiftieth wedding anniversary.

THANKS FOR

taking the time to find

out what's really

important to me.

Thanks for running
back upstairs to change
before the party when
I arrived at your house
in the same dress you
were wearing.

Thanks for loaning me your grandmother's ivory linen tablecloth for my holiday brunch.

THANKS FOR

never laying a guilt

trip on me.

THANKS FOR

always returning my

sunglasses when I leave

them in your car.

Thanks for
having the extra dime
for the pay phone.

Thanks for starting
the community watch
program in our area.

THANKS FOR

being the best "block Mom"

in our neighborhood.

THANKS FOR

telling me my dark blue

eyeshadow was a

bit too retro.

Thanks for
helping me polish
my grandmother's
good silver.

Thanks for fixing a
casserole and bringing
some over for my family
on soccer night.

THANKS FOR

bringing me tomatoes

from your garden

every summer.

THANKS FOR

making homemade

ice cream.

Thanks for
not being
two-faced.

Thanks for never
saying hurtful things,
even accidentally.

THANKS FOR

treasuring our time together.

THANKS FOR

serving me decaf coffee

after four in the afternoon.

290

Thanks for
valuing my opinion
when you're making
tough life decisions.

Thanks for
your forgiveness.

THANKS FOR

saving all the bows from my

wedding shower and making

a pillow from them for my

tenth wedding anniversary.

THANKS FOR

taking a picture of a rainbow

and sending it to me.

Thanks for
the authentic beret
you brought me
from Paris.

Thanks for
always telling me
the juicy gossip.

THANKS FOR

not laughing when I cried

through the whole movie.

THANKS FOR

recommending a

wonderful hairstylist.

Thanks for saving me from the goofy guy in the nightclub.

Thanks for
helping me make
my mom's birthday
so special.

THANKS FOR

always sending me thank-you

notes for little things I do.

THANKS FOR

explaining the rules of

the baseball game so I would

know what was going on.

Thanks for
helping me think of
fun things to cook for
my family reunion.

Thanks for rushing
to the emergency room
with me when my
daughter broke her arm.

THANKS FOR

reading between the lines.

THANKS FOR

buying me shots at my

bachelorette party.

306

Thanks for
missing me when we
don't see each other
for a while.

Thanks for
reading the map
when we go on
our day trips.

THANKS FOR

proofreading my résumé.

THANKS FOR

using your real china teacups

when I come over.

Thanks for reminding me
that with all its faults,
this is a beautiful
world we live in.

Thanks for
helping me can
my tomatoes.

THANKS FOR

bringing over brownies

when I first moved

in next door.

THANKS FOR

ordering dessert with

two spoons.

Thanks for loaning me
the nail polish in your purse
when my panty hose ran.

Thanks for
being my muse.

316

THANKS FOR

really connecting with me.

THANKS FOR

giving me reasons to take

vacation days from work.

318

Thanks for taking
dance lessons with me.

Thanks for
recommending a
fun baby-sitter
for my kids.

THANKS FOR

getting excited about my

accomplishments.

THANKS FOR

showing me that going gray

isn't the end of the world.

Thanks for being totally
involved in my life.

Thanks for
going overboard,
just for fun.

THANKS FOR

making sure the train

on my wedding gown

looked picture-perfect.

THANKS FOR

being my chemistry tutor

in college.

Thanks for pushing me
to be my best.

Thanks for not
being a hypocrite.

THANKS FOR

running to the store for

candles when we needed

them for my fiancé's

surprise birthday party.

THANKS FOR

carrying my lawn chair when

my hands were full at the Fourth

of July fireworks display.

Thanks for
the back rubs.

Thanks for coming
to get me when I was
stranded in the middle of
the night and not asking
any questions.

THANKS FOR

telling me when you were just

two weeks pregnant.

THANKS FOR

giving me a journal to keep

track of my thoughts.

Thanks for pinning the straps of my new dress when they broke during our senior prom.

Thanks for the
gift certificate to the
day spa for my
thirtieth birthday.

THANKS FOR

loaning me your antique

cradle for my baby.

THANKS FOR

helping me put together

a care package to cheer up

my daughter during finals.

Thanks for driving
the four hours to my house
just so we could see each
other before you had to fly
home with your family.

Thanks for bailing me
out of jail when I got
arrested at the protest.

THANKS FOR

convincing me not to

cut my long hair.

THANKS FOR

letting me use your computer

when mine went kaput.

Thanks for
always providing
stimulating conversation.

Thanks for
sharing every stage
of my life.

THANKS FOR

loving my cat as

much as I do.

THANKS FOR

being my oldest friend.

Thanks for always having a vegetarian dish for me at your dinner parties.

Thanks for
typing my paper
for me in college
while I slept.

THANKS FOR

making ordinary situations

seem funny.

THANKS FOR

knocking on my apartment

door and inviting me to

go for walks with you.

Thanks for
knowing what I mean
when I give you that
wink over a crowd.

Thanks for
always having your
camera to capture our
adventures on film.

THANKS FOR

swimming laps with me.

THANKS FOR

going canoeing with me.

Thanks for
not noticing the
few pounds I put on
over the winter.

Thanks for painting
my toenails when we
were in a hurry to
be somewhere.

THANKS FOR

saving me a seat for

lunch in high school.

THANKS FOR

curling the back of my

hair when it was too short

for me to reach.

Thanks for
getting the gum out
of my hair at the
ball game.

Thanks for
teaching me my first
swear word when
we were kids.

THANKS FOR

putting the worm on

the hook when my dad

took us fishing.

THANKS FOR

singing along when our favorite

song comes on the radio.

Thanks for
getting my favorite
pro football player's
autograph for me.

Thanks for
being so chatty.

THANKS FOR

buying the sound tracks

to our favorite movies so we

can listen to them together.

THANKS FOR

being the best friend

I could have in college.

Thanks for
helping make our
college dorm room
look like home.

Thanks for being you.

THANKS FOR

pointing out the rainbow

after the storm.

Thanks for
being my friend.